BARITONE T.C.

BROADWAY FAVORITES

Solos and Band Arrangements
Correlated with Essential Elements Band Method

Arranged by
MICHAEL SWEENEY

Welcome to Essential Elements Broadway Favorites! There are two versions of each selection in this versatile book. The SOLO version appears in the beginning of each student book. The FULL BAND arrangements of each song follows. The supplemental CD recording or PIANO ACCOMPANIMENT BOOK may be used as an accompaniment for solo performance. Use these recordings when playing solos for friends and family.

ISBN 978-0-7935-9854-0

HAL•LEONARD®
CORPORATION

7777 W. BLUEMOUND RD. P.O. BOX 13819 MILWAUKEE, WI 53213

Copyright © 1998 by HAL LEONARD CORPORATION
International Copyright Secured   All Rights Reserved

00860048

From Walt Disney's BEAUTY AND THE BEAST: THE BROADWAY MUSICAL

BEAUTY AND THE BEAST

BARITONE T.C.
SOLO

Lyrics by HOWARD ASHMAN
Music by ALAN MENKEN
Arranged by MICHAEL SWEENEY

© 1991 Walt Disney Music Company and Wonderland Music Company, Inc.
This arrangement © 1998 Walt Disney Music Company, Inc. and Wonderland Music Company, Inc.
All Rights Reserved   Used by Permission

From the Musical Production ANNIE

TOMORROW

BARITONE T.C.
Solo

Lyric by MARTIN CHARNIN
Music by CHARLES STROUSE
Arranged by MICHAEL SWEENEY

© 1977, 1998 EDWIN H. MORRIS & COMPANY, A Division of MPL Communications, Inc. and CHARLES STROUSE
All Rights Reserved

0860048

From the Musical CABARET

CABARET

Words by FRED EBB
Music by JOHN KANDER
Arranged by MICHAEL SWEENEY

BARITONE T.C.
Solo

Copyright © 1966, 1967 by Alley Music Corp. and Trio Music Co., Inc.
Copyright Renewed
This arrangement Copyright © 1998 by Alley Music Corp. and Trio Music Co., Inc.
International Copyright Secured   All Rights Reserved
Used by Permission

00860048

From THE SOUND OF MUSIC
EDELWEISS

BARITONE T.C.
Solo

Lyrics by OSCAR HAMMERSTEIN II
Music by RICHARD RODGERS
Arranged by MICHAEL SWEENEY

Copyright © 1959 by Richard Rodgers and Oscar Hammerstein II
Copyright Renewed
This arrangement Copyright © 1998 by WILLIAMSON MUSIC
WILLIAMSON MUSIC owner of publication and allied rights throughout the world
International Copyright Secured   All Rights Reserved

From EVITA
DON'T CRY FOR ME ARGENTINA

BARITONE T.C.
Solo

Words by TIM RICE
Music by ANDREW LLOYD WEBBER
Arranged by MICHAEL SWEENEY

© Copyright 1976, 1977 by EVITA MUSIC LTD.
This arrangement © Copyright 1998 by EVITA MUSIC LTD.
All Rights for the USA and Canada Controlled and Administered by MCA - ON BACKSTREET MUSIC, INC.
International Copyright Secured   All Rights Reserved

00860048

MCA Music Publishing

GET ME TO THE CHURCH ON TIME

BARITONE T.C.
Solo

Words by ALAN JAY LERNER
Music by FREDERICK LOEWE
Arranged by MICHAEL SWEENEY

Copyright © 1956 by Alan Jay Lerner and Frederick Loewe
Copyright Renewed
This arrangement Copyright © 1998 by Alan Jay Lerner and Frederick Loewe
Chappell & Co. owner of publication and allied rights throughout the world
International Copyright Secured   All Rights Reserved

00860048

From LES MISÉRABLES

I DREAMED A DREAM

Music by CLAUDE-MICHEL SCHÖNBERG
Lyrics by ALAIN BOUBLIL,
JEAN-MARC NATEL and HERBERT KRETZMER
Arranged by MICHAEL SWEENEY

BARITONE T.C.
Solo

Play lower notes if possible

Music and French Lyrics Copyright © 1980 by Editions Musicales Alain Boublil
English Lyrics Copyright © 1986 by Alain Boublil Music Ltd. (ASCAP)
This edition Copyright © 1998 by Alain Boublil Music Ltd. (ASCAP)
Mechanical and Publication Rights for the U.S.A. Administered by Alain Boublil Music Ltd. (ASCAP)
c/o Spielman Koenigsberg & Parker LLP, Richard Koenigsberg, 1745 Broadway, New York NY 10019, Tel 212-453-2500, Fax 212-453-2550, ABML@skpny.com
International Copyright Secured. All Rights Reserved. This music is copyright. Photocopying is illegal.
All Performance Rights Restricted.

From JOSEPH AND THE AMAZING TECHNICOLOR DREAMCOAT

GO GO GO JOSEPH

BARITONE T.C.
Solo

Music by ANDREW LLOYD WEBBER
Lyrics by TIM RICE
Arranged by MICHAEL SWEENEY

© Copyright 1969 The Really Useful Group Ltd.
Copyright Renewed
This arrangement © Copyright 1998 The Really Useful Group Ltd.
All Rights for North America Controlled by Williamson Music Co.
International Copyright Secured   All Rights Reserved

From CATS
MEMORY

BARITONE T.C.
Solo

Music by ANDREW LLOYD WEBBER
Text by TREVOR NUNN after T.S. ELIOT
Arranged by MICHAEL SWEENEY

Music Copyright © 1981 The Really Useful Group Ltd.
Text Copyright © 1981 Trevor Nunn and Set Copyrights Ltd.
This arrangement Copyright © 1998 The Really Useful Group Ltd.
All Rights for The Really Useful Group Ltd. for the United States and Canada Administered by Songs Of PolyGram International, Inc.
All Rights in the text Controlled by Faber and Faber Ltd. and Administered for the United States and Canada by R&H Music Co.
International Copyright Secured   All Rights Reserved

THE PHANTOM OF THE OPERA

BARITONE T.C.
Solo

Music by ANDREW LLOYD WEBBER
Lyrics by CHARLES HART
Additional Lyrics by RICHARD STILGOE and MIKE BATT
Arranged by MICHAEL SWEENEY

© Copyright 1986 The Really Useful Group Ltd.
This arrangement © Copyright 1998 The Really Useful Group Ltd.
All Rights for the United States and Canada Administered by PolyGram International Publishing, Inc.
International Copyright Secured   All Rights Reserved

From Meredith Willson's THE MUSIC MAN

SEVENTY SIX TROMBONES

By MEREDITH WILLSON
Arranged by MICHAEL SWEENEY

BARITONE T.C.
Solo

© 1957 (Renewed) FRANK MUSIC CORP. and MEREDITH WILLSON MUSIC
This arrangement © 1998 FRANK MUSIC CORP. and MEREDITH WILLSON MUSIC
All Rights Reserved

From Walt Disney's BEAUTY AND THE BEAST: THE BROADWAY MUSICAL

BEAUTY AND THE BEAST

Lyrics by HOWARD ASHMAN
Music by ALAN MENKEN
Arranged by MICHAEL SWEENEY

BARITONE T.C.
Band Arrangement

© 1991 Walt Disney Music Company and Wonderland Music Company, Inc.
This arrangement © 1998 Walt Disney Music Company, Inc. and Wonderland Music Company, Inc.
All Rights Reserved   Used by Permission

From the Musical Production ANNIE

TOMORROW

BARITONE T.C.
Band Arrangement

Lyric by MARTIN CHARNIN
Music by CHARLES STROUSE
Arranged by MICHAEL SWEENEY

© 1977, 1998 EDWIN H. MORRIS & COMPANY, A Division of MPL Communications, Inc. and CHARLES STROUSE
All Rights Reserved

From the Musical CABARET
CABARET

Words by FRED EBB
Music by JOHN KANDER
Arranged by MICHAEL SWEENEY

BARITONE T.C.
and Arrangement

Copyright © 1966, 1967 by Alley Music Corp. and Trio Music Co., Inc.
Copyright Renewed
This arrangement Copyright © 1998 by Alley Music Corp. and Trio Music Co., Inc.
International Copyright Secured   All Rights Reserved
Used by Permission

From THE SOUND OF MUSIC
EDELWEISS

BARITONE T.C.
Band Arrangement

Lyrics by OSCAR HAMMERSTEIN II
Music by RICHARD RODGERS
Arranged by MICHAEL SWEENEY

Copyright © 1959 by Richard Rodgers and Oscar Hammerstein II
Copyright Renewed
This arrangement Copyright © 1998 by WILLIAMSON MUSIC
WILLIAMSON MUSIC owner of publication and allied rights throughout the world
International Copyright Secured   All Rights Reserved

From EVITA

DON'T CRY FOR ME ARGENTINA

BARITONE T.C.
Band Arrangement

Words by TIM RICE
Music by ANDREW LLOYD WEBBER
Arranged by MICHAEL SWEENEY

© Copyright 1976, 1977 by EVITA MUSIC LTD.
This arrangement © Copyright 1998 by EVITA MUSIC LTD.
All Rights for the USA and Canada Controlled and Administered by MCA - ON BACKSTREET MUSIC, INC.
International Copyright Secured   All Rights Reserved

From MY FAIR LADY

GET ME TO THE CHURCH ON TIME

BARITONE T.C.
Band Arrangement

Words by ALAN JAY LERNER
Music by FREDERICK LOEWE
Arranged by MICHAEL SWEENEY

Copyright © 1956 by Alan Jay Lerner and Frederick Loewe
Copyright Renewed
This arrangement Copyright © 1998 by Alan Jay Lerner and Frederick Loewe
Chappell & Co. owner of publication and allied rights throughout the world
International Copyright Secured   All Rights Reserved

00860048

I DREAMED A DREAM

BARITONE T.C.
Band Arrangement

Music by CLAUDE-MICHEL SCHÖNBERG
Lyrics by ALAIN BOUBLIL,
JEAN-MARC NATEL and HERBERT KRETZMER

Arranged by MICHAEL SWEENEY

Music and French Lyrics Copyright © 1980 by Editions Musicales Alain Boublil
English Lyrics Copyright © 1986 by Alain Boublil Music Ltd. (ASCAP)
This edition Copyright © 1998 by Alain Boublil Music Ltd. (ASCAP)
Mechanical and Publication Rights for the U.S.A. Administered by Alain Boublil Music Ltd. (ASCAP)
c/o Spielman Koenigsberg & Parker LLP, Richard Koenigsberg, 1745 Broadway, New York NY 10019, Tel 212-453-2500, Fax 212-453-2550, ABML@skpny.com
International Copyright Secured. All Rights Reserved. This music is copyright. Photocopying is illegal.
All Performance Rights Restricted.

860048

From JOSEPH AND THE AMAZING TECHNICOLOR DREAMCOAT

GO GO GO JOSEPH

BARITONE T.C.
Band Arrangement

Music by ANDREW LLOYD WEBBER
Lyrics by TIM RICE
Arranged by MICHAEL SWEENEY

© Copyright 1969 The Really Useful Group Ltd.
Copyright Renewed
This arrangement © Copyright 1998 The Really Useful Group Ltd.
All Rights for North America Controlled by Williamson Music Co.
International Copyright Secured   All Rights Reserved

00860048

From CATS
MEMORY

BARITONE T.C.
Band Arrangement

Music by ANDREW LLOYD WEBBER
Text by TREVOR NUNN after T.S. ELIOT
Arranged by MICHAEL SWEENEY

Music Copyright © 1981 The Really Useful Group Ltd.
Text Copyright © 1981 Trevor Nunn and Set Copyrights Ltd.
This arrangement Copyright © 1998 The Really Useful Group Ltd.
All Rights for The Really Useful Group Ltd. for the United States and Canada Administered by Songs Of PolyGram International, Inc.
All Rights in the text Controlled by Faber and Faber Ltd. and Administered for the United States and Canada by R&H Music Co.
International Copyright Secured   All Rights Reserved

860048

From THE PHANTOM OF THE OPERA

THE PHANTOM OF THE OPERA

Music by ANDREW LLOYD WEBBER
Lyrics by CHARLES HART
Additional Lyrics by RICHARD STILGOE and MIKE BATT
Arranged by MICHAEL SWEENEY

BARITONE T.C.
Band Arrangement

© Copyright 1986 The Really Useful Group Ltd.
This arrangement © Copyright 1998 The Really Useful Group Ltd.
All Rights for the United States and Canada Administered by PolyGram International Publishing, Inc.
International Copyright Secured   All Rights Reserved

00860048

From Meredith Willson's THE MUSIC MAN

SEVENTY SIX TROMBONES

By MEREDITH WILLSON
Arranged by MICHAEL SWEENEY

BARITONE T.C.
Band Arrangement

© 1957 (Renewed) FRANK MUSIC CORP. and MEREDITH WILLSON MUSIC
This arrangement © 1998 FRANK MUSIC CORP. and MEREDITH WILLSON MUSIC
All Rights Reserved

860048